Dedicated with love to
the Anderson family.

TOOTS and PLOPS

Written by CAVE
Illustrated by Jasmine Wibbens

P.U.!

Was that you?

Mommy smells a stinky toot. Your tummy might be telling you it's time to sit on the potty and poop.

Pull your pants down
and climb on up!

Let's see if your body makes a
TOOT or a PLOP.

Listen for the sound
your poop makes
when it drops!

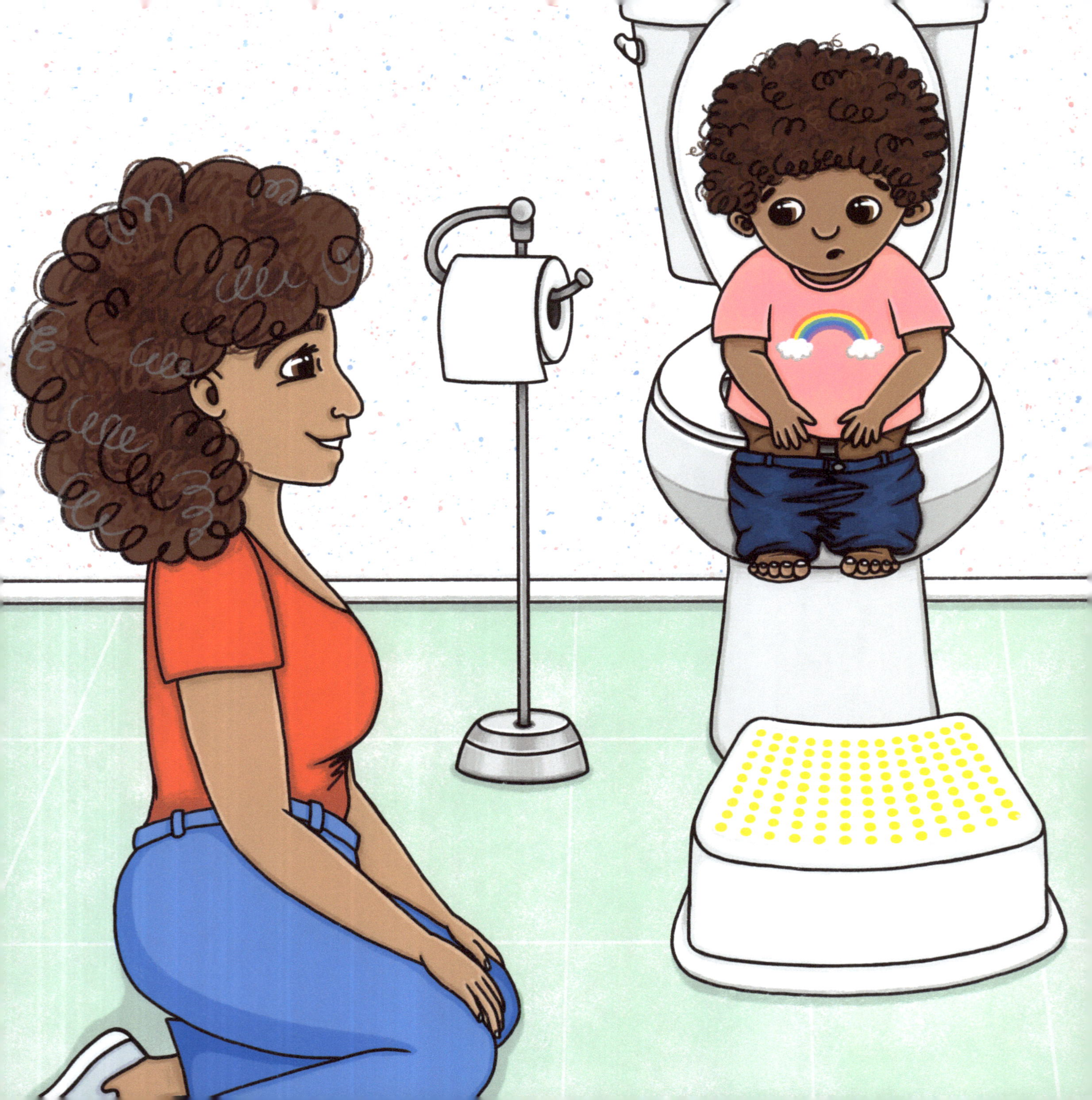

How many plops
do you think there
will be?

One? Two?
Maybe even three?

Push out
your poops
and count
with me...

TOOTS and PLOPS and PLOPS and TOOTS...

Pooping on the potty
is good for you!

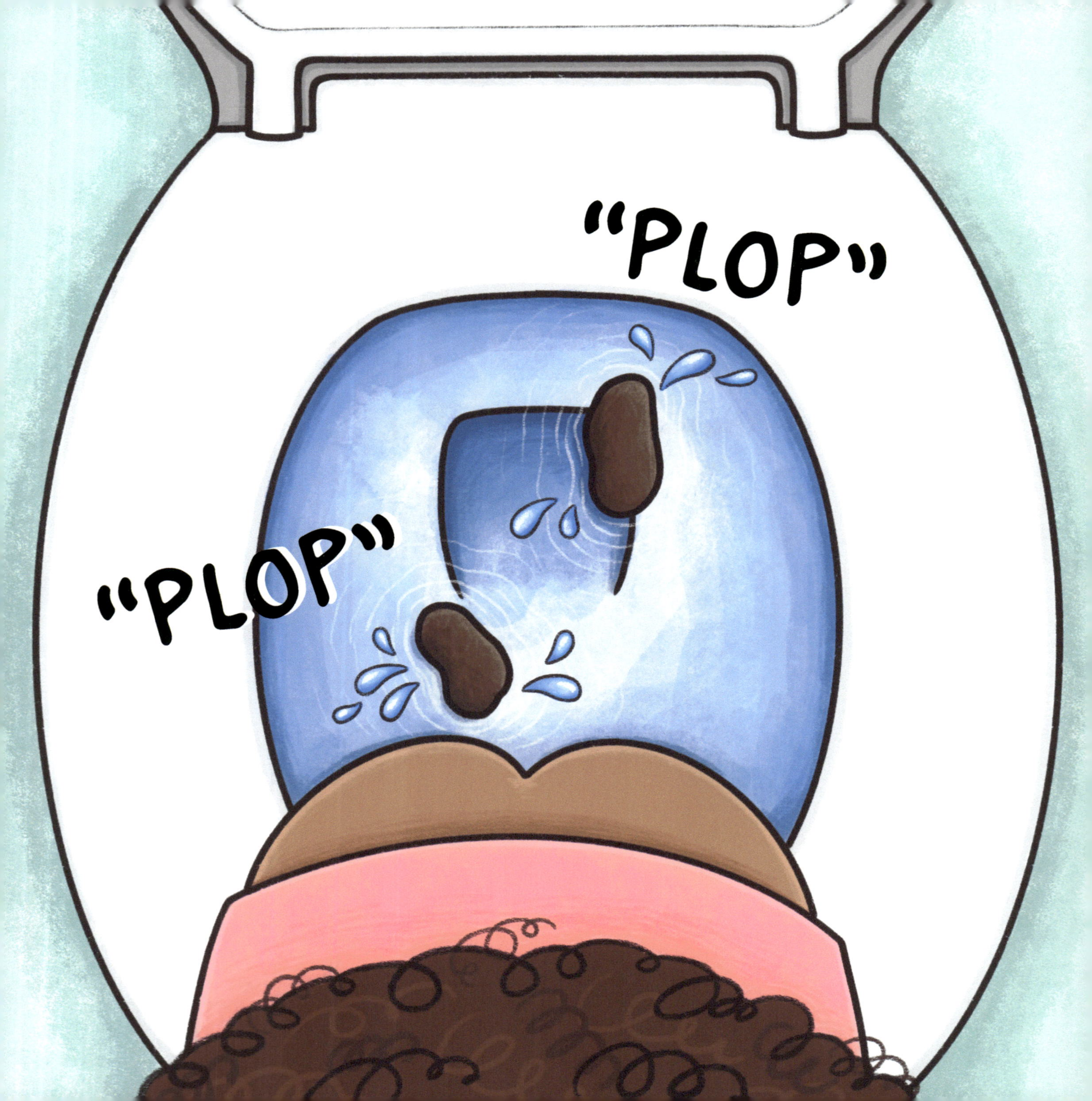

"PLOP"
"PLOP"

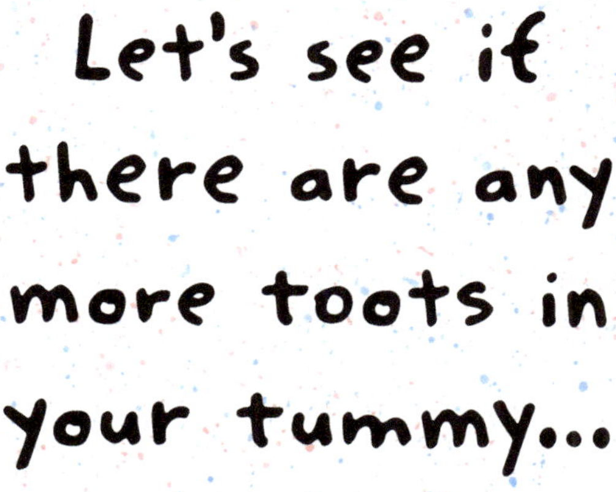

Whoa! Two!
Great job honey!

Let's see if there are any more toots in your tummy...

TOOT!

Phew!
What a
silly sound!

Now let's wipe
your bum and
flush your
poop down

There! All done.
Counting plops was fun!

I'm proud of you
for going potty.

Well done.

PLOPS and TOOTS
and
TOOTS and PLOPS...
TOOT!

Listen for the sound
your poop makes
when it drops!

TOOTS and PLOPS and PLOPS and TOOTS...

Pooping on the potty is
so good for you!